D0382498

TITLE I
HOLMES JR HIGH
2001-02

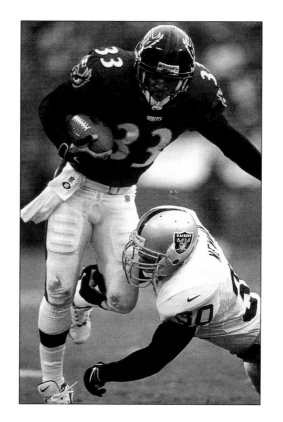

CREATIVE EDUCATION

BALTIMORE RAVENS

JOHN NICHOLS

Published by Creative Education
123 South Broad Street, Mankato, Minnesota 56001
Creative Education is an imprint of The Creative Company

Designed by Rita Marshall

Photos by: Allsport USA, SportsChrome

Library of Congress Cataloging-in-Publication Data

Nichols, John, 1966–
Baltimore Ravens / by John Nichols.
p. cm. — (NFL today)
Summary: Traces the history of this team from its transformation from the
Cleveland Browns to the Baltimore Ravens in 1996 through the 1999 season.
ISBN 1-58341-036-8

1. Baltimore Ravens (Football team)—Juvenile literature. [1. Baltimore Ravens
(Football team)—History. 2. Football—History.] I. Title. II. Series: NFL today
(Mankato, Minn.)

GV956.B35N53   2000
796.357'64'097526—dc21   99-041021

First edition

9 8 7 6 5 4 3 2 1

Baltimore, the largest city in the state of Maryland, is also one of the busiest seaports in the United States. Located on beautiful Chesapeake Bay, Baltimore has been a prominent commercial center since colonial times. As late as 1850, Baltimore was the second-largest metropolis in the entire country, trailing only New York City in population.

Baltimore is known for its bustling harbor, but it has also played a major role in American history. Francis Scott Key composed the "Star-Spangled Banner," the United States' national anthem, at Baltimore's Fort McHenry in 1814. The lyrics to the anthem were inspired by Key's first-hand view-

Baltimore's beautiful PSINet Stadium.

ing of a decisive battle during the War of 1812, when a British fleet bombarded the fort in an unsuccessful attempt to capture it and the city of Baltimore.

Another part of Baltimore's rich history involves its famous sports teams. In major league baseball, the Baltimore Orioles have consistently been one of the most competitive franchises in the American League for more than four decades. In the National Football League, the old Baltimore Colts were one of the great teams from 1953 until 1984—when they moved to Indianapolis.

1 9 9 6

Tough safety Eric Turner played in the Pro Bowl after making 112 tackles.

The Colts' move broke the hearts of Baltimore football fans. But in late 1995, fans received the good news that the NFL was returning to Baltimore. The Cleveland Browns announced that the team would become the Baltimore Ravens for the 1996 season and would occupy a new football stadium to be built near Oriole Park at Camden Yards, the state-of-the-art baseball complex.

Baltimore fans have good reason to celebrate after only a few seasons. Their young football team already has several of the NFL's most exciting players dotting its roster. Rising stars such as Jonathan Ogden, Michael McCrary, and Peter Boulware have the Baltimore faithful excited about a football future that could be even greater than its past.

THE RAVENS ARE HATCHED

When team owner Art Modell decided to move the Cleveland Browns to Baltimore, he knew he was moving to a city that loved its football. The Baltimore Colts had been one of the most beloved and successful franchises

Fierce linebacker Jamie Sharper.

Fans counted on head coach Ted Marchibroda to make the Ravens into contenders.

in the sport's history. But when the team packed up and moved to Indianapolis in 1984, Baltimore fans were left with no one to cheer for.

In February 1996, all of that would change. Modell received permission from the NFL to move the Browns from the shores of Lake Erie to Baltimore. Modell had decided to move the Browns after the city of Cleveland refused to build a new stadium to replace the aging Cleveland Stadium. Feeling his team could no longer compete financially if located in Cleveland, Modell moved to Baltimore, where a new stadium would be built.

Because the city of Cleveland kept the rights to the Browns' team name, history, and colors, the new Baltimore team would basically be starting over. "I wanted the fans in Cleveland to have what belonged to them," Modell said. "The Browns' name and everything that goes along with it will stay in Cleveland." In March 1996, an extensive search for Baltimore's new nickname ended. A 33,000-vote poll determined that Maryland's new football team would be called the "Ravens."

A raven is a large black bird that often appears purple in the sunlight. One of Baltimore's most famous citizens, author Edgar Allen Poe, portrayed a talking raven as the title character in "The Raven," one of his best-known poems. "It gives us a strong nickname that is not common to teams at any level [of competition], and it gives us one that means something to our community," said team executive David Modell.

The new Ravens would have a familiar face to guide them from the sidelines. Ted Marchibroda, who coached the old Baltimore Colts from 1975 to 1979, would be the Ravens' first head coach. Coincidentally, Marchibroda was brought to Baltimore after guiding the Indianapolis Colts from 1992 to 1995. "To come home to Baltimore means so much to me and my family," said Marchibroda. "I know what football means to this community, and to be a part of the NFL's return here is something I would have never predicted."

1 9 9 6

Veteran running back Earnest Byner contributed 904 yards on runs and pass receptions.

OGDEN AND LEWIS LAY THE FOUNDATION

Marchibroda's challenge would be to turn around a team that had stumbled to a 5–11 mark in its last season in Cleveland. Marchibroda recognized the franchise's desperate need for young talent. "We're looking to find some impact players in the draft," the new coach explained. "We need to find people that we can put at a position and leave there for 10 years."

Marchibroda took a huge step in the right direction in the Ravens' first draft in 1996. With its two first-round picks, the team plucked prized players Jonathan Ogden and Ray Lewis from the college ranks.

The 6-foot-8 and 325-pound Ogden was rated by many scouts as the best player available in the draft. The mountainous offensive lineman had been absolutely dominant in his final two seasons at UCLA, allowing only two quarterback sacks. "Ogden is a physical marvel," gushed one scout. "He's so big, and yet he is so quick and explosive. Plus he's a real smart kid."

Ogden, who had won the Outland Trophy as the nation's best college lineman, was forced to make an early adjustment with the Ravens. Although he had played tackle for

Vinny Testaverde passed for 7,148 yards in two seasons in Baltimore.

Receiver Derrick Alexander keyed a deadly air attack.

Antonio Langham led the team with five interceptions and 21 total passes defensed.

most of his college career, Ogden moved inside to play left guard for Baltimore. "I thought of it as a challenge," said Ogden. "If I was going to play guard, I was going to be the best guard I could be."

On the defensive side, the Ravens used the 26th overall pick to take Ray Lewis, a tough linebacker out of the University of Miami. Lewis gave the Ravens a big defender who could cover a lot of ground and deliver plenty of crushing hits. "On all the film we watched, we never saw Ray ever take a play off," noted Ravens defensive coordinator Marvin Lewis. "He never got tired and he never backed down. You could see he loved playing linebacker."

In his first season, Ogden quickly proved to be one of the league's best young linemen as he steamrolled opposing defenders and earned a spot on the NFL's All-Rookie team. Sparked by the giant's stellar play, the Ravens emerged as one of the league's most explosive offenses in 1996. Quarterback Vinny Testaverde, running backs Bam Morris and Earnest Byner, and receivers Michael Jackson and Derrick Alexander paced a Baltimore attack that rolled up an average of 358 yards a game—third-best in the NFL.

Lewis also made a big impression in his rookie year. In addition to his team-leading 142 tackles, he contributed 2.5 sacks and an interception from his inside linebacker position. Lewis racked up the strong numbers as several of the Ravens' starting defensive linemen went down with injuries, leaving him with little help against the run.

The Ravens' first season was characterized by offensive fireworks for both Baltimore and its opponents. With a potent offense and a crippled defense, the Ravens were forced to try to outscore opponents in shootouts, a strategy that produced mixed results. Quarterback Vinny Testaverde's 33 touchdown passes earned him a spot in the Pro Bowl, but the Ravens suffered through a difficult 4–12 season.

"GOOSE" AND BOULWARE BOLSTER THE DEFENSE

As the 1997 season approached, Coach Marchibroda's main goal was to upgrade a defense that had given up an average of 28 points a game in 1996. Linebacker Ray Lewis and veteran safety Eric Turner had been outstanding, but the Ravens needed more talent. "We certainly didn't play as well defensively as we would have liked," Marchibroda said. "We got a rash of injuries, and we couldn't overcome it."

Safety Stevon Moore made 86 tackles and forced two fumbles.

Massive nose tackle Tony Siragusa.

Linebacker Peter Boulware's 11.5 sacks earned him Defensive Rookie of the Year honors.

The Ravens strengthened their defensive line by luring free agent nose tackle Tony Siragusa away from the Indianapolis Colts. The 6-foot-3 and 320-pound "Goose," as Siragusa is called by fans and teammates, gave Baltimore the big run-stuffer they needed to help control opposing running attacks. Marchibroda was thrilled to add the veteran to his roster. "He's been to the playoffs," the coach explained. "He knows what it takes to win. He is a character guy and a character performer."

Siragusa added brawn to the Ravens' defense, but the unit also needed to add some speed and pass-rushing ability. Baltimore had managed only 30 quarterback sacks its first season and had given up a league-worst 248 yards a game through the air. "We need to get to the quarterback and knock him down," Marchibroda summed up. "The best pass defense in the world is a big rush, and we lacked that our first year."

To change that, the Ravens chose Florida State linebacker Peter Boulware with their first-round pick in the 1997 draft. The 6-foot-4 and 255-pound Boulware had drawn raves from scouts with his rare combination of size and speed. After the Ravens selected Boulware with the fourth overall pick, NFL draft expert Mel Kiper noted, "Boulware is big enough to stuff the run, fast enough to cover backs, and skilled enough to be one heck of a pass rusher. This is exactly what the doctor ordered for Baltimore."

In 1997, Siragusa used his immense strength and big body to neutralize blockers, often bringing opposing running games to a standstill. With the Goose clogging up the middle of the line, the Ravens' run defense improved dramatically.

All-Pro offensive tackle Jonathan Ogden.

Running back Bam Morris left tacklers bruised and battered.

"Tony doesn't pile up a lot of stats," said Ray Lewis. "He just does all the dirty work so the rest of us can run to the ball and make tackles. He keeps all those big bodies off me."

Boulware turned out to be just as big of a boost for the Ravens' pass rush. Though he often had to fight double- and sometimes triple-team blocking, the rookie linebacker stormed through opposing lines to record 11.5 quarterback sacks—only one sack short of the NFL rookie record. "He has a chance to be a top-flight pass rusher in this league for a lot of years," noted Tennessee Titans head coach Jeff Fisher. "I don't think you compare him to anybody else—we'll be comparing other players to him."

Despite their much-improved defense, the Ravens improved their record in 1997 to only 6–9–1. An inconsistent offense and untimely turnovers caused the Ravens to lose seven games by eight points or less. Ozzie Newsome, the Ravens' vice president of player personnel and former Cleveland Browns great, blamed Baltimore's youth for the team's lack of success in close games. "We've got a lot of young guys playing big roles on this team," Newsome noted. "They are still learning what it takes to close the show in the fourth quarter."

1 9 9 7

End Michael McCrary finished the season with a career-high 80 defensive stops.

NEW NEST FOR THE RAVENS

In the Ravens' first two seasons, home games were played at Memorial Stadium, the former home of the Colts. Although the Ravens did not win many games in their first two years, they always defended their home turf with a vengeance. Of the 10 wins the team compiled in 1996 and

The anchor of the defense, Ray Lewis (pages 18-19).

1997, seven of them came in front of the roaring crowds at Memorial Stadium.

While the Ravens appreciated the glorious past of Memorial Stadium and had some success there, they anxiously awaited the day they would have a place to call their own. "We've enjoyed playing in the old stadium," said Marchibroda. "It brought back a lot of memories. But this is a different team and a different time. We can't wait to get in our new stadium."

1 9 9 8

Jim Harbaugh threw for nearly 2,000 yards in his 12 games as the Ravens' starter.

The new stadium Marchibroda was referring to was the $220-million facility being built next to the Baltimore Orioles' baseball park at Camden Yards. Under construction during the Ravens' first two seasons, the new stadium was finally completed in time for the 1998 campaign. The Ravens' new nest—named PSINet Stadium—is a glittering example of modern architecture. More than 185 feet tall, the huge, natural-grass facility provides seating for 68,400 fans and features 108 luxury suites.

Ravens players saw the stadium as the beginning of a new chapter in Baltimore football. "Playing at Memorial Stadium was great, but you sort of felt the place wasn't really ours," said wide receiver Michael Jackson. "It still sort of belonged to the old Colts. This place is all ours."

As they prepared to leave Memorial Stadium for their new home, the Ravens brought in several new players, including veteran quarterback Jim Harbaugh and seven-time Pro-Bowl cornerback Rod Woodson. The 35-year-old Harbaugh and 33-year-old Woodson were proven winners with long careers, and Baltimore fans hoped they could provide the veteran leadership that the young Ravens had been lacking.

"Jim and Rod aren't 25 anymore, and we don't expect them to carry the load for us," explained Ozzie Newsome. "But these guys have been able to lift the teams they played on to a higher level. We think that will happen here."

Harbaugh battled nagging injuries in 1998, throwing 12 touchdowns but also 11 interceptions. The ageless Woodson logged another productive season, leading the Baltimore defense by intercepting six passes—two of which he returned for touchdowns.

Despite the two veterans' efforts, the Ravens finished the '98 season with another disappointing 6–9–1 record. The team's offense sputtered, and the overworked defense wore down by the season's end. "We thought this would be a breakthrough year for us, and it didn't happen," team owner

1 9 9 8

Jermaine Lewis averaged 19.1 yards per catch and scored on two punt returns.

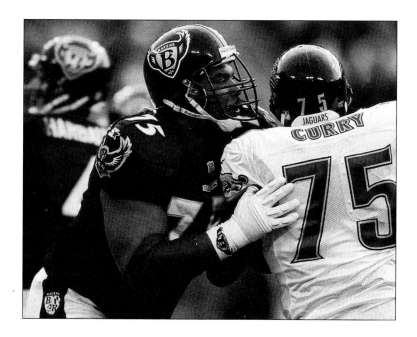

Gigantic lineman Jonathen Ogden.

21

Tight end Eric Green was a reliable passing target.

Art Modell said with frustration. "The time has come for us to move in a different direction." After the 1998 season, Ted Marchibroda was fired as head coach.

BILLICK TAKES CONTROL

Errict Rhett was part of a Ravens backfield that pounded out 1,629 rushing yards.

The Ravens' point-scoring woes in 1998 led them to look for an offense-oriented head coach to replace Ted Marchibroda. After interviewing several prospects, Baltimore chose Minnesota Vikings offensive coordinator Brian Billick to be the team's new head man.

During his five years with the Vikings, Billick had earned a reputation as one of the brightest offensive minds in the league. He had been responsible for guiding one of the NFL's most fearsome attacks, expertly blending the talents of such Vikings stars as receivers Cris Carter and Randy Moss and quarterback Randall Cunningham to form a nearly unstoppable offensive machine.

In 1998, Billick's Vikings offense set a new NFL record for most points scored in a season with 556, breaking the old mark set by the 1983 Washington Redskins. "Brian has a great ability to get the most out of his guys," said Billick's former boss, Vikings head coach Dennis Green. "He's very bright and imaginative. He deserves a chance to lead a team."

Baltimore got a first-hand look at Billick's offensive genius when the Ravens hosted the Vikings late in the 1998 season. Baltimore scored 28 points but still came up short in a 38–28 decision, as the Vikings rolled up 420 yards in total offense. "We had identified Brian as one of the top young coaches in the game," Ravens owner Art Modell said, "but after that performance, we became convinced that he would be our top choice once the season was over."

Billick also came away from the game with a favorable impression of Baltimore. "I remember looking up and thinking what a great place to play football this is," he said. "The stadium is first-class, the fans fill the stands even though the team has not won much, and the players all seemed to have so much spirit. I liked what I saw."

At the press conference announcing his hiring, Coach Billick told Baltimore reporters he was ready for the challenge. "I've prepared to be an NFL head coach, and I'm ready," he said. "I like the talent on this team, and I feel that Ozzie Newsome and I can find the rest of the pieces to get this franchise over the hump."

1 9 9 9

New coach Brian Billick was hired to rebuild the Ravens' sagging offense.

Strong-legged kicker Matt Stover.

Upon taking control of the Ravens, new head coach Brian Billick began looking to add more speed on both sides of the ball. "In order to attack on both offense and defense, we need to get faster," noted Billick. "Team speed is going to be one of our building blocks."

On offense, the Ravens already had speed to burn in wide receiver and kick returner Jermaine Lewis. The 1996 fifth-round draft pick from the University of Maryland began his pro career slowly. He caught only five passes as a rookie but opened many eyes around the league with his slick moves and blazing speed as a kick and punt returner. Although the 5-foot-7 and 172-pound Lewis is a pint-sized receiver in a league of giants, he has never considered his size a disadvantage. "I've been the smallest guy on every football team I've ever played on," Lewis said. "The defensive backs are always telling me how they are going to bust me up. All I ever say is, 'first you have to catch me.'"

Defenders around the league soon learned that catching the speedy Lewis is easier said than done. In 1997, he led the NFL in yards per punt return and set an NFL record by returning two punts for touchdowns in one game against the Seattle Seahawks. Lewis also began to show his brilliance as a wide receiver in 1998, catching 41 passes for 784 yards and six touchdowns. "Jermaine is one dangerous guy," Brian Billick said. "We have to find ways to get the ball into his hands as much as we can."

To help move the ball, the Ravens also looked to halfback Priest Holmes for solid production on the ground. The shifty

1 9 9 9

Qadry Ismail posted a team record with 1,105 receiving yards.

Relentless defensive end Michael McCrary (pages 26-27).

Holmes became the first 1,000-yard rusher in Ravens history when he ran for 1,008 yards and seven touchdowns in 1998.

On defense, Baltimore added speed to their deep patrol by drafting University of Arizona cornerback Chris McAlister with their top pick in the 1999 NFL draft. The 6-foot-1 and 205-pound defensive back combined with Duane Starks to give the Ravens two fast young corners capable of shutting down dangerous opposing receivers. "Chris is big and strong and will be able to battle all the tall receivers that are so common in today's game," Billick predicted. "He's what we mean by bringing in people who can make the big play."

The addition of McAlister allowed the Ravens to move Rod Woodson from cornerback to safety, firming up another position on their roster. "We need to get better in all facets of

1 9 9 9

Linebacker Jamie Sharper emerged as a defensive star, making 95 tackles.

Aggressive cornerback Chris McAlister.

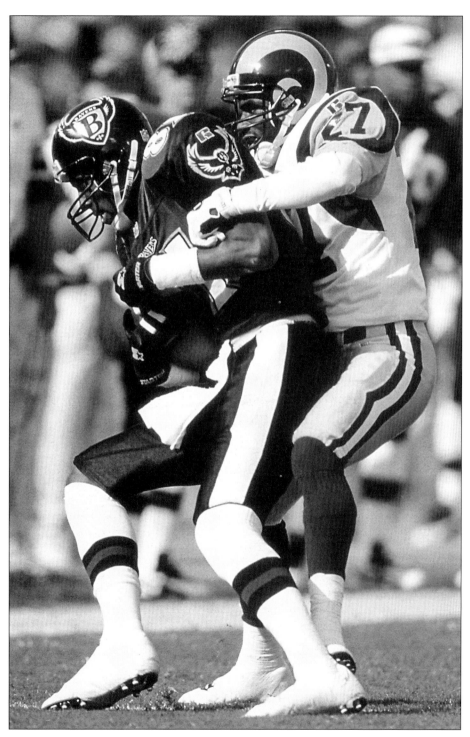

Game-breaking wide receiver Michael Jackson.

Explosive offensive star Jermaine Lewis.

Feared pass rusher Peter Boulware.

The Ravens expect- ed All-Pro Shannon Sharpe to make big contributions to their offense.

the game," stated Billick before the team's first mini-camp. "I don't believe this is a 6–10 team. I know we're better than that. Every guy on this team better believe it too."

Wins wouldn't come easily early on for Billick's Ravens. After seven games, the team's record stood at a woeful 2–5. The offense struggled with Scott Mitchell at quarterback, and he was eventually replaced by strong-armed Tony Banks.

Banks had had a short and inconsistent career with the St. Louis Rams. His tremendous potential had caught Billick's eye, however, and he was brought to Baltimore as a third-string quarterback. When the team's first two quarterbacks fizzled, Banks was inserted into the starting lineup. Almost instantly, the Ravens offense began to take flight. Banks's powerful arm and solid decision-making blended perfectly with Billick's attacking philosophy, and the Ravens began to roll.

Over the season's last nine games, the Ravens averaged 25 points a contest while winning six games and losing two others by a total of six points. Banks's 17 touchdown passes, in a little more than half a season, gave the Ravens an offense mighty enough to compare to its ferocious defense. "We leaned on our defense early on when we couldn't do anything offensively," observed Coach Billick. "It's nice to reward those men for never quitting."

The Ravens' late-season surge came too late for them to make the playoffs, but Billick's team appears ready to make its mark on the league. With a roster featuring a wealth of rising stars on both sides of the ball, it may only be a matter of time before the Ravens soar to the top of the NFL.